ESSENTIAL ELEMENTS®

GUITAR ENSEMBLES

TURBO ROCK

10 ORIGINAL SONGS WITH POWER CHORDS AND RIFFS

by Mark Huls

T0081520

ISBN-13: 978-1-4234-2545-8
ISBN-10: 1-4234-2545-6

HAL•LEONARD® CORPORATION

7777 W. BLUEMOUND RD. P.O. BOX 13819 MILWAUKEE, WI 53213

In Australia Contact:
Hal Leonard Australia Pty. Ltd.
4 Lentara Court
Cheltenham, Victoria, 3192 Australia
Email: ausadmin@halleonard.com

Visit Hal Leonard Online at
www.halleonard.com

PREFACE

My parents believed in the discipline of music. I began playing guitar at age 13, motivated by father's desire to see me doing something other than hanging out with the local neighborhood kids and getting into trouble. I think he was also inspired by the idea of a father and son activity and a notion of trying his hand at learning the guitar. That lasted about two weeks, so I was left alone in the hands of a beautiful blonde guitar teacher named Beth Love. She was a rocker to the core.

Learning open position chords and other guitar basics quickly gave way to power chords and the first rock song I ever played, "Rock You Like a Hurricane" by the Scorpions. I was stoked. The power chord movements in that song, along with the rhythm, were easy and fun. They were also powerful and driving enough to motivate a 13-year-old student to become a guitar player for life. So, when the folks at Hal Leonard presented me with the idea of writing the exercises for this book, I was happy to accept their offer.

Turbo Rock is a collection of ten songs in the hard rock style of such bands as AC/DC, Ozzy, Rage Against the Machine, and Tool—to name a few. Often, when a guitar student who is a fan of hard rock begins to learn the instrument, it can be difficult to find songs with the drive and intensity of the style that are simple enough to play. The book you hold in your hands was written for that very reason.

Rock is so cool. It is an integral part of the guitar experience. I've enjoyed writing and playing the pieces in this book. I hope you have fun with them, too, and that they make your introduction to the guitar a more rocking one.

Thanks, Dad and Beth.

–Mark Huls

CONTENTS

BLUE STEAM
By Mark Huls

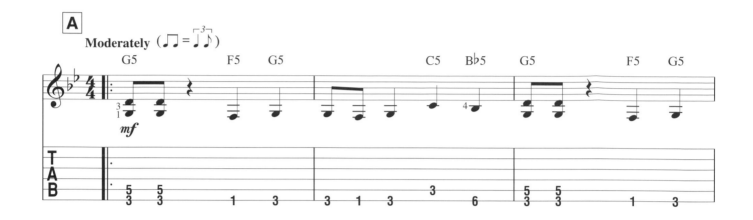

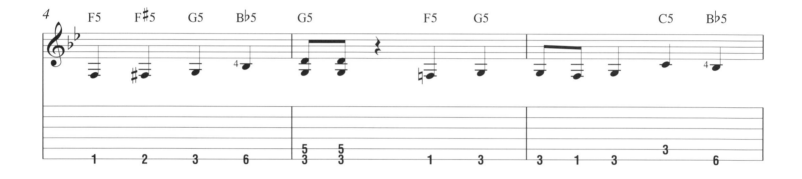

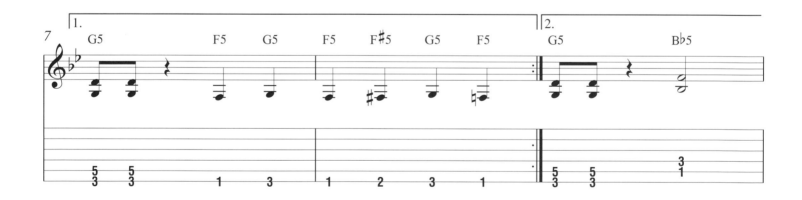

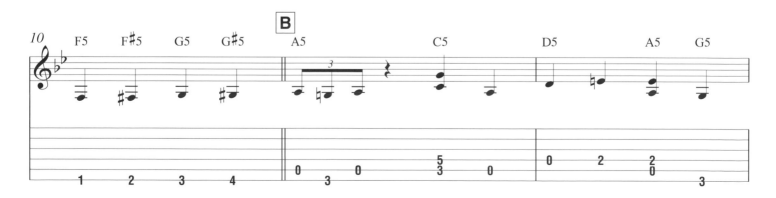

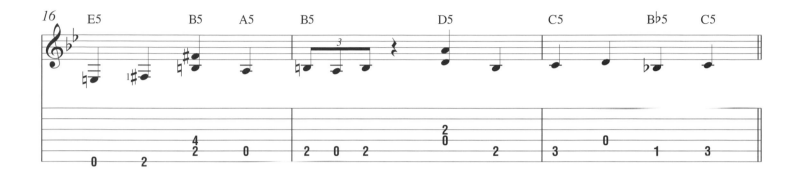

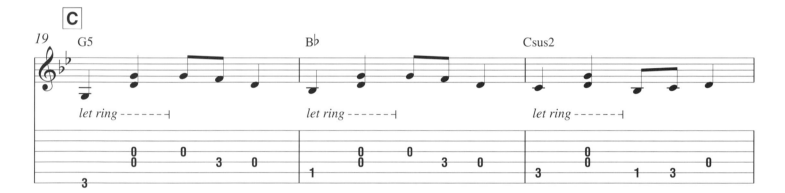

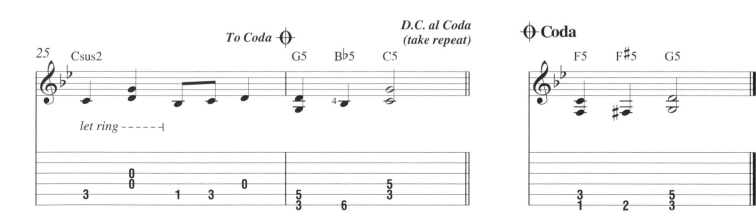

CHAIN REACTION

By Mark Huls

TRACK 2

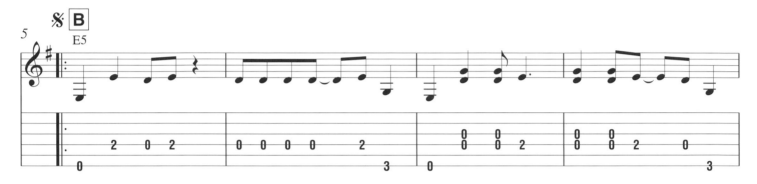

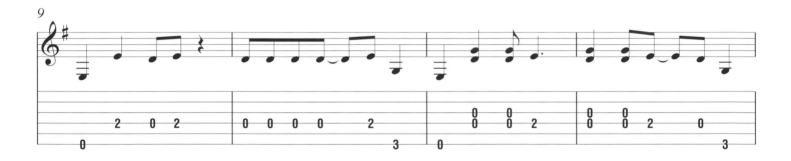

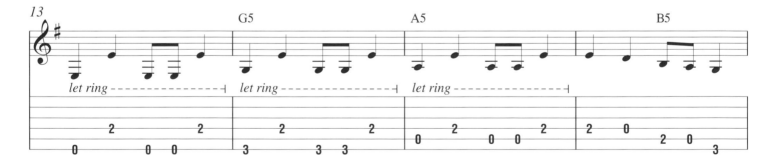

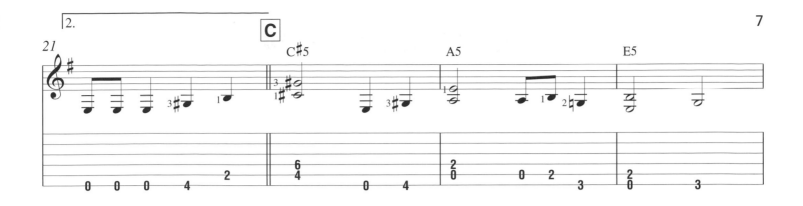

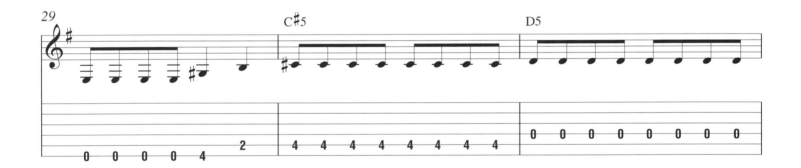

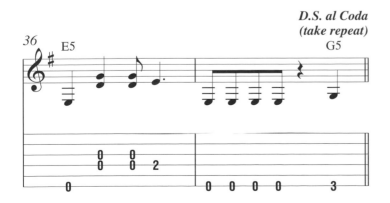

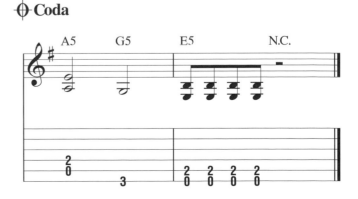

TRACK 3

DR. GRIND
By Mark Huls

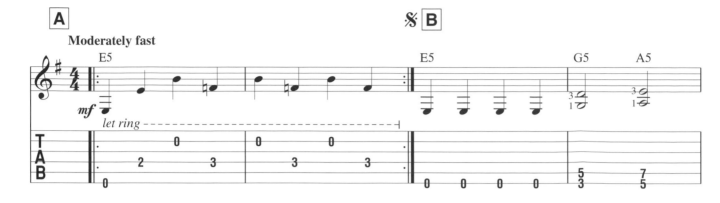

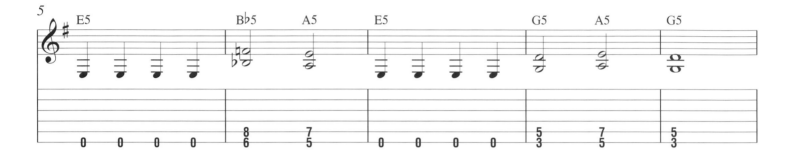

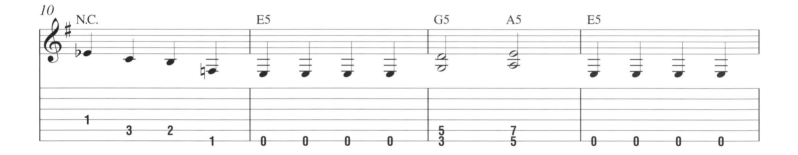

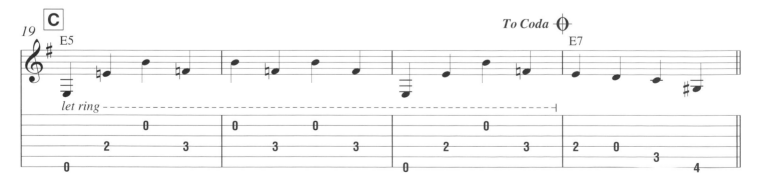

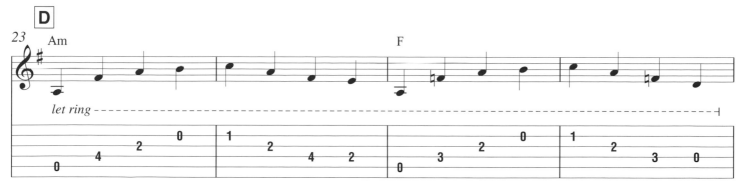

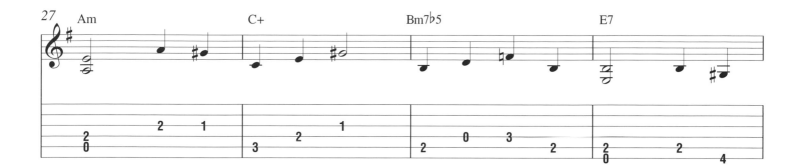

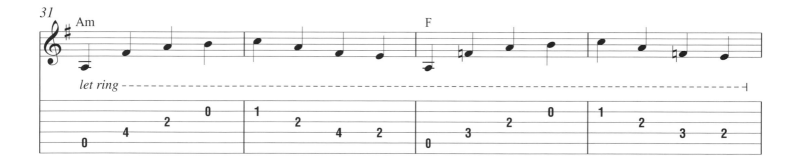

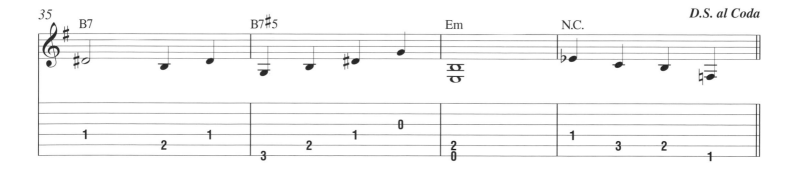

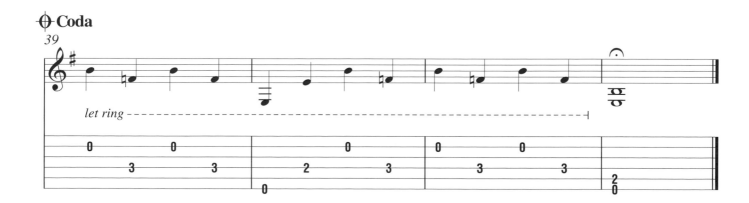

DRIVE
By Mark Huls

TRACK 4

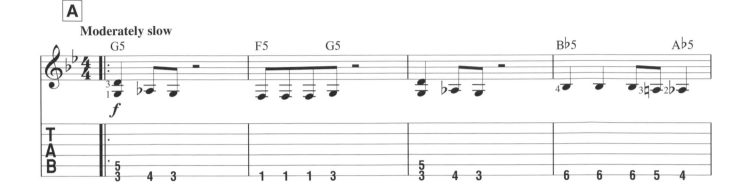

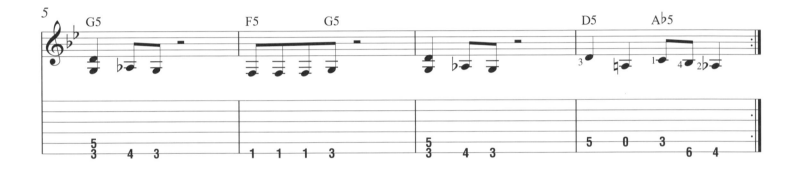

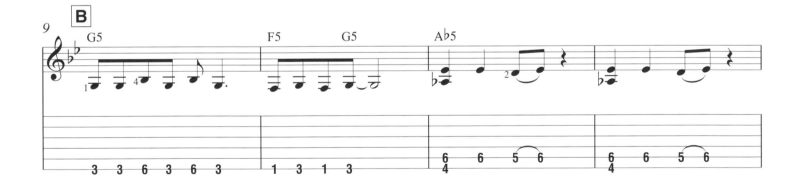

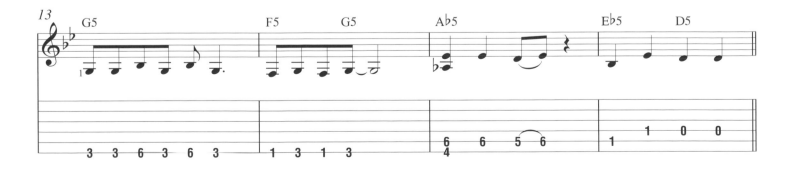

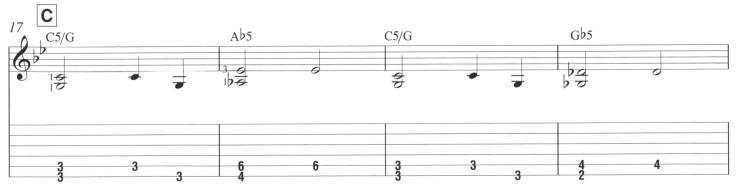

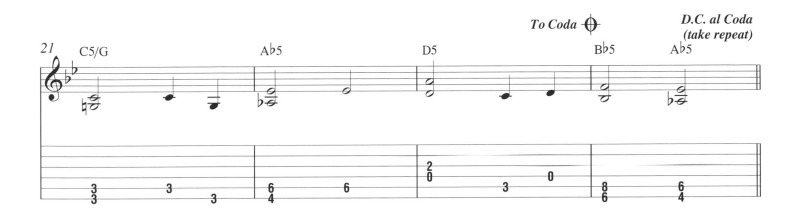

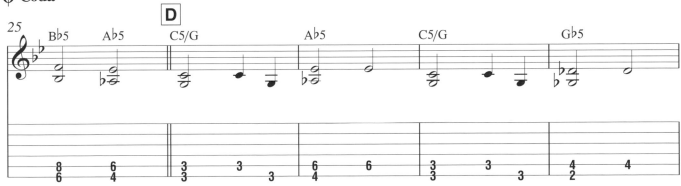

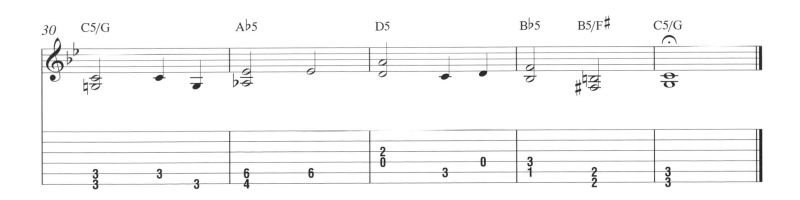

FALLOUT
By Mark Huls

TRACK 5

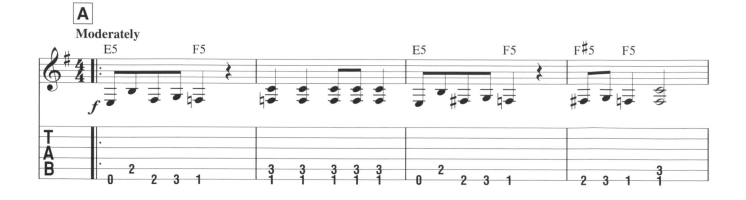

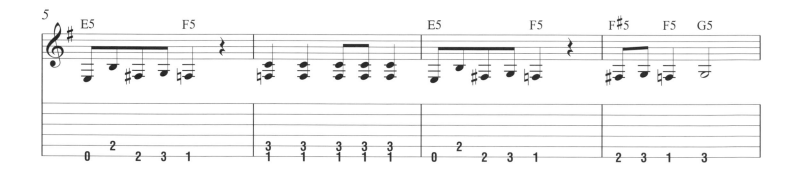

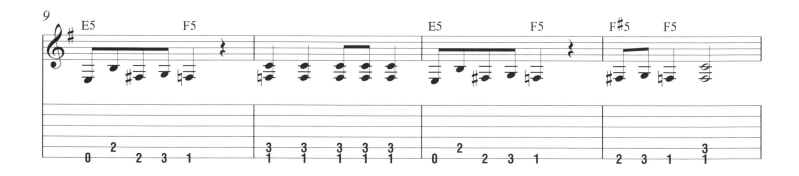

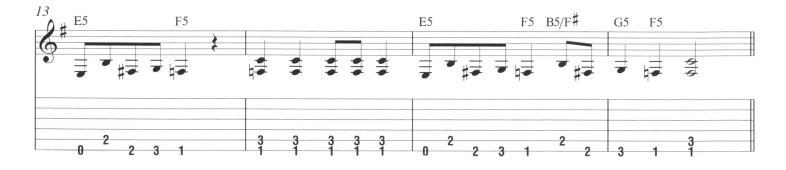

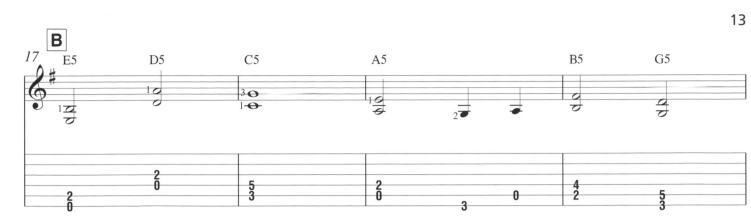

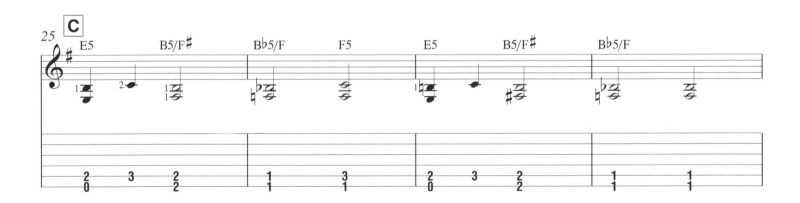

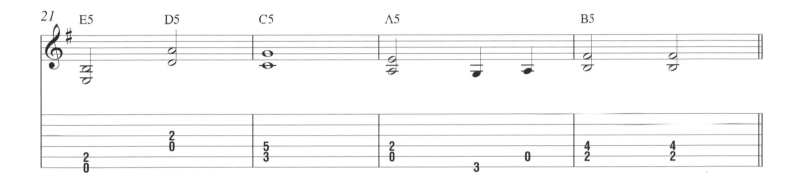

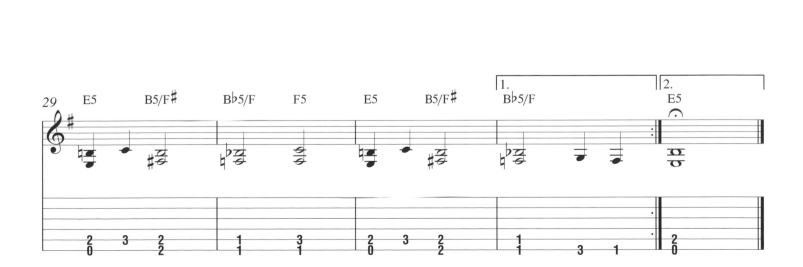

THE FRINGE

By Mark Huls

TRACK 6

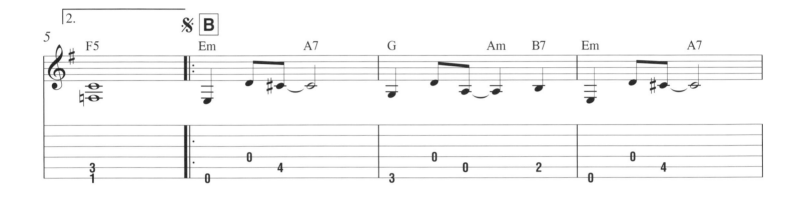

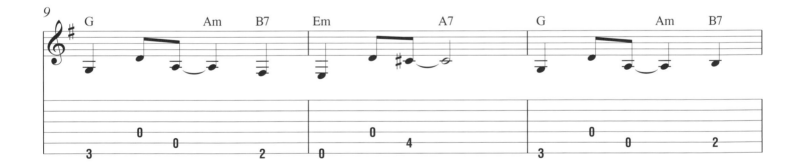

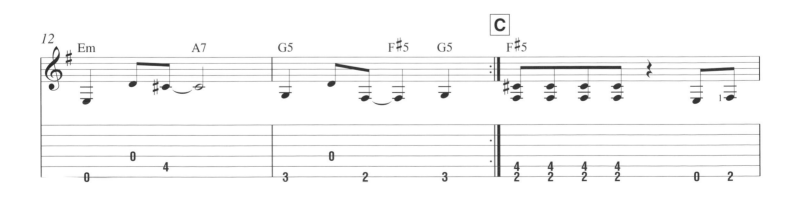

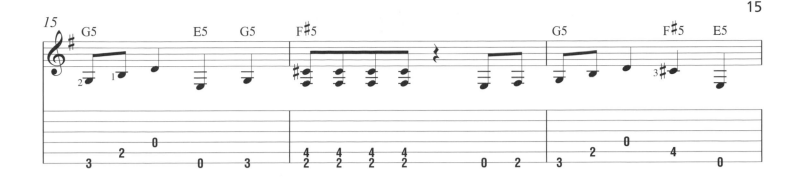

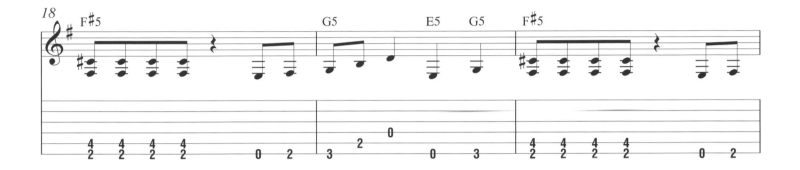

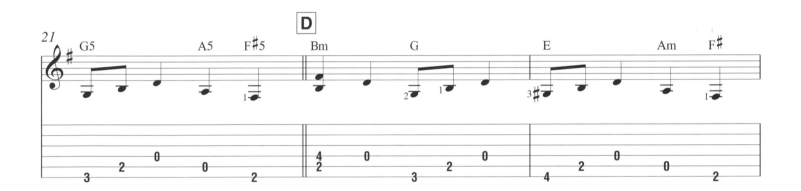

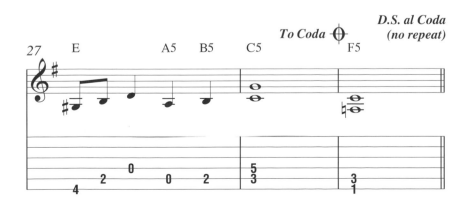

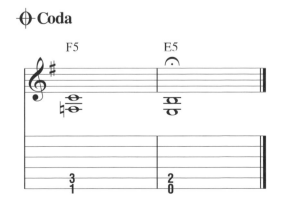

LIVE WIRE

By Mark Huls

TRACK 7

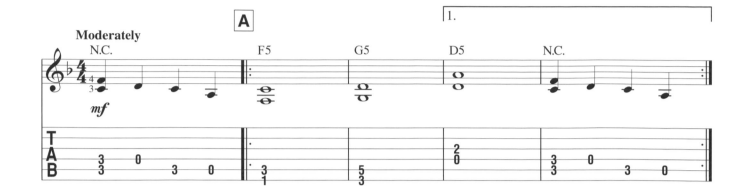

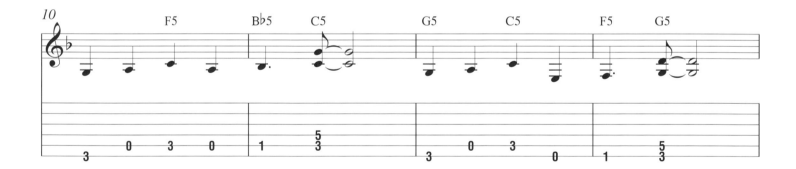

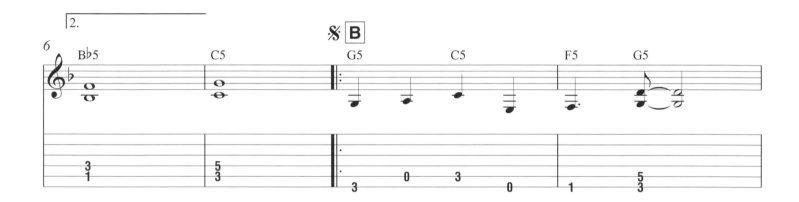

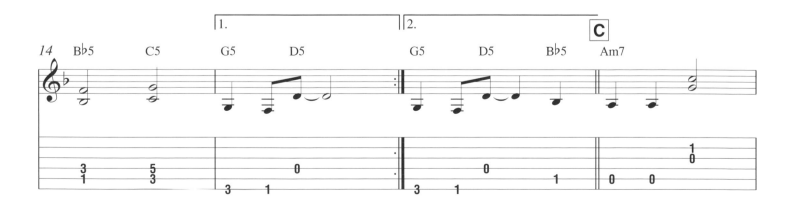

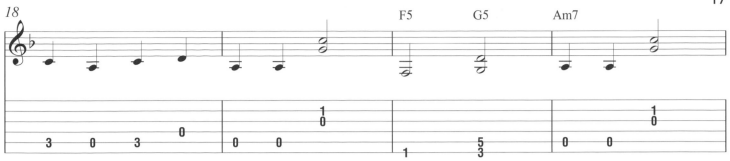

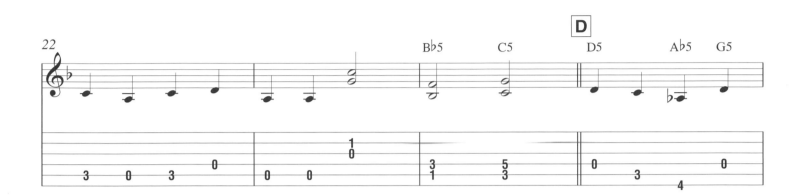

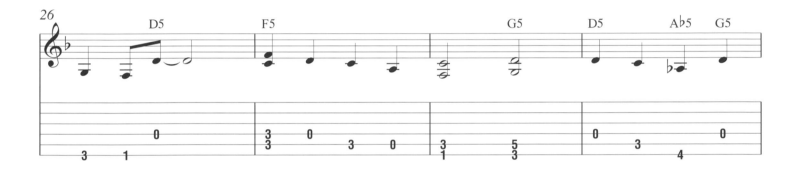

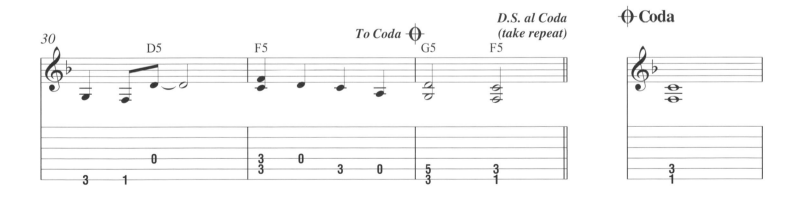

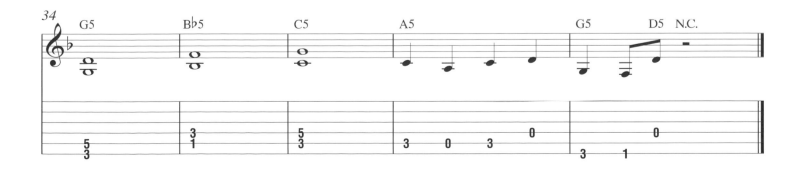

TRACK 8

A RUMBLE AND A HUM
By Mark Huls

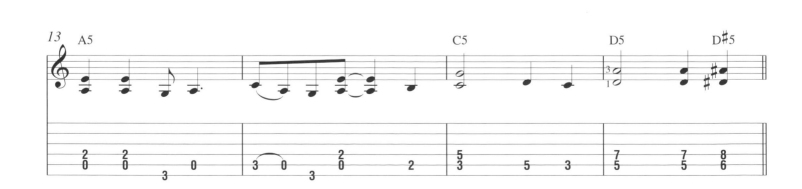

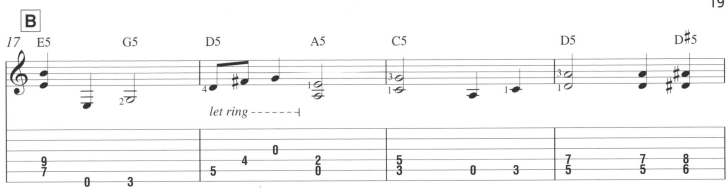

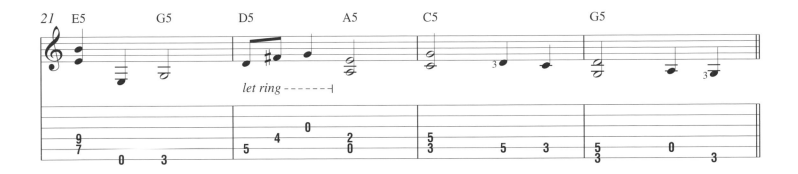

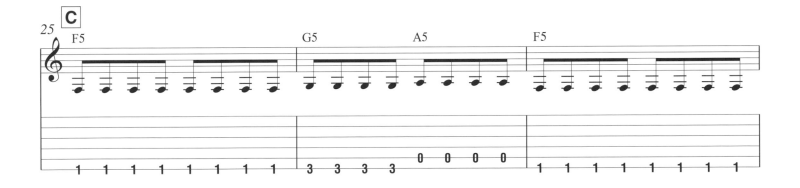

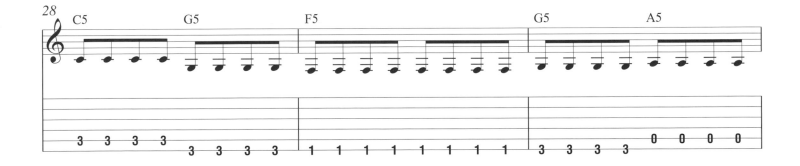

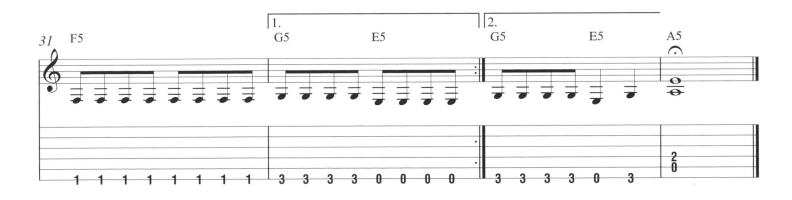

SLOW BURN

By Mark Huls

TRACK 9

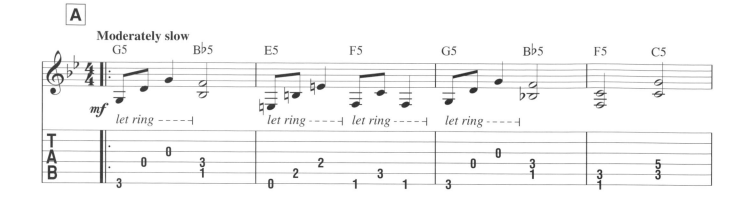

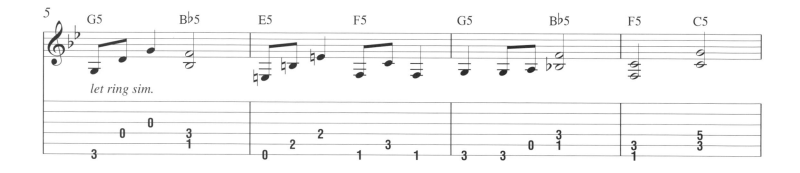

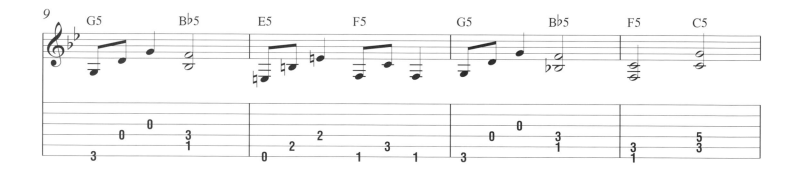

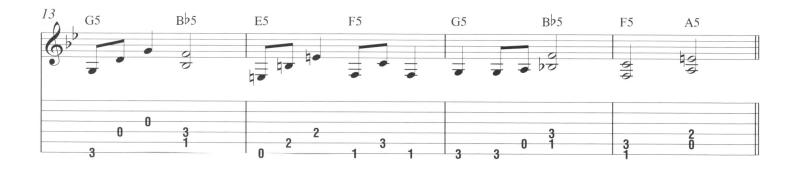

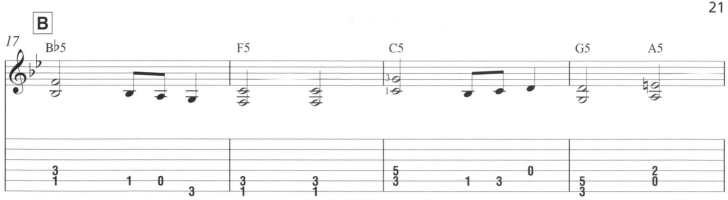

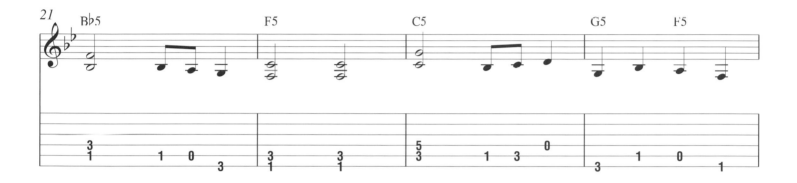

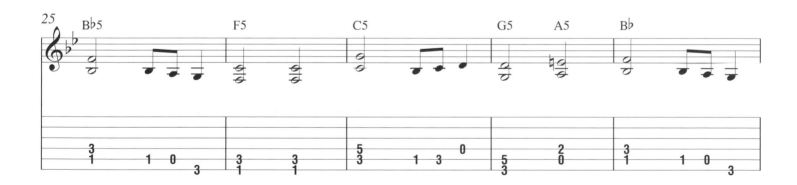

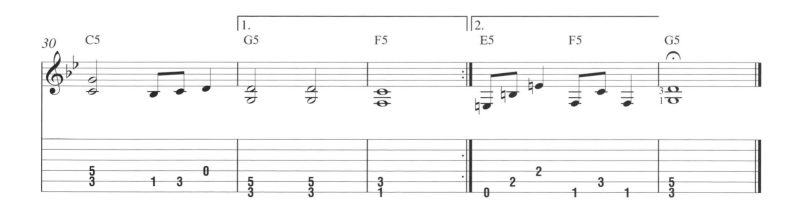

TURBO ROCK
By Mark Huls

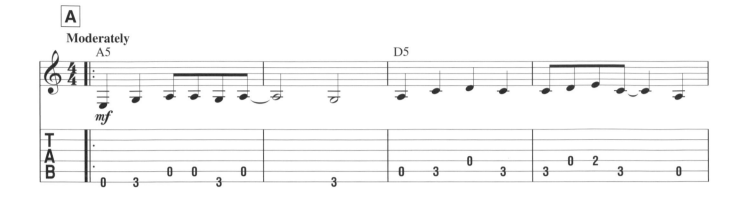

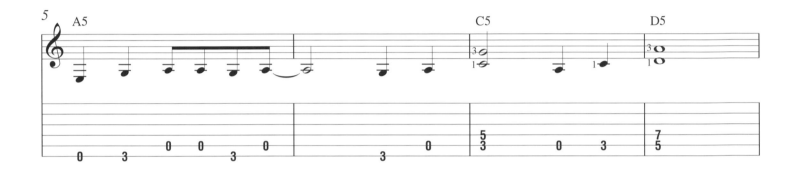

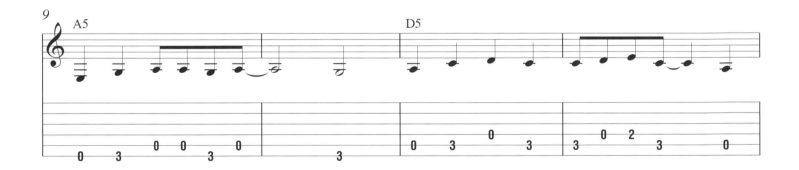

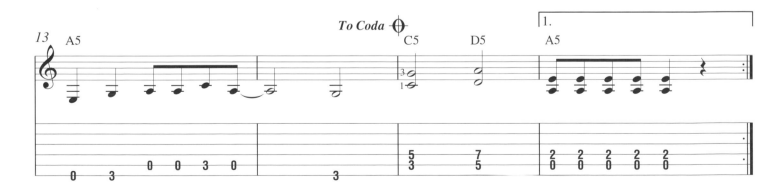

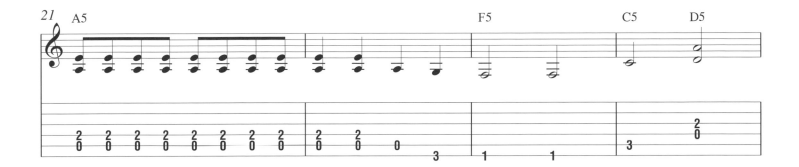

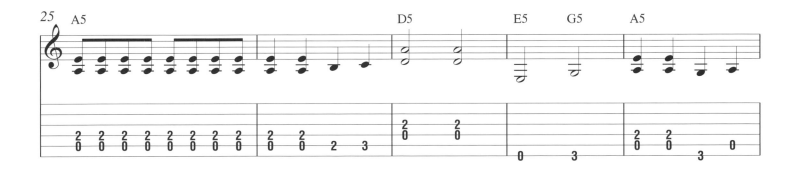

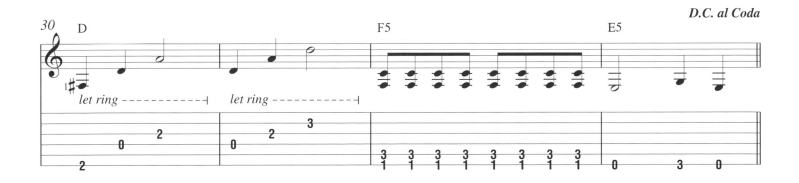

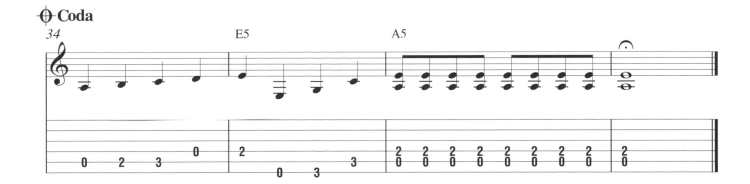

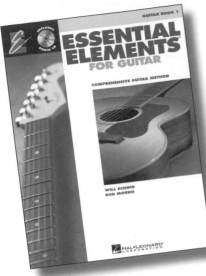

ESSENTIAL ELEMENTS FOR GUITAR, BOOK 1

Comprehensive Guitar Method
by Will Schmid and Bob Morris

Take your guitar teaching to a new level! Hal Leonard's top-selling comprehensive method for band and strings is now also available for guitar. With the time-tested classroom teaching methods of Will Schmid and Bob Morris, popular songs in a variety of styles, and quality demonstration and backing tracks on the accompanying CD, *Essential Elements for Guitar* is sure to become a staple of guitar teachers' instruction – and get beginning guitar students off to a great start.

This method has been designed to meet the National Standards for Music Education, with features such as cross-curricular activities, quizzes, multicultural songs, basic improvisation and more. Concepts covered in Book 1 include: getting started; basic music theory; guitar chords; notes on each string; music history; ensemble playing; performance spotlights; and much more!

Songs used in Book 1 include such hits as: Dust in the Wind • Eleanor Rigby • Every Breath You Take • Hey Jude • Hound Dog • Let It Be • Ode to Joy • Rock Around the Clock • Stand by Me • Surfin' USA • Sweet Home Chicago • This Land Is Your Land • You Really Got Me • and more!

00862639 Book/CD Pack...$17.95

Essential Elements Guitar Ensembles

The songs in Hal Leonard's Essential Elements Guitar Ensemble series are playable by multiple guitars. Each arrangement features the melody (lead), a harmony part, and a bass line. Chord symbols are also provided if you wish to add a rhythm part. For groups with more than three or four guitars, the parts may be doubled. Play all of the parts together, or record some of the parts and play the remaining part along with your recording. All of the songs are printed on two facing pages; no page turns are required. This series is perfect for classroom guitar ensembles or other group guitar settings.

CHRISTMAS SONGS

15 Holiday Hits Arranged for Three or More Guitarists

Songs include: Blue Christmas • The Christmas Song • Christmas Time Is Here • Do You Hear What I Hear • Frosty the Snow Man • Here Comes Santa Claus (Right Down Santa Claus Lane) • A Holly Jolly Christmas • I'll Be Home for Christmas • Jingle-Bell Rock • Let It Snow! Let It Snow! Let It Snow! • My Favorite Things • Rockin' Around the Christmas Tree • Rudolph the Red-Nosed Reindeer • Santa Claus Is Comin' to Town • Silver Bells.
00001136...$9.95

POP HITS

15 Pop Hits Arranged for Three or More Guitarists

Songs include: Best of My Love • Brown Eyed Girl • Dreams • Dust in the Wind • Every Breath You Take • I Get Around • Imagine • Let It Be • My Cherie Amour • Oh, Pretty Woman • Stand by Me • Still the Same • Wonderful Tonight • Y.M.C.A. • Your Song.
00001128 ....$9.95

Essential Elements Guitar Repertoire Series

Hal Leonard's Essential Elements Guitar Repertoire Series features great original guitar music based on a style or theme that is carefully graded and leveled for easy selection. The songs are presented in standard notation and tablature, and are fully demonstrated on the accompanying CD.

TURBO ROCK

Beginner Intermediate Level
by Mark Huls

Turbo Rock features 10 original songs with power chords and riffs. Includes: Blue Steam • Chain Reaction • Dr. Grind • Drive • Fallout • The Fringe • Live Wire • A Rumble and a Hum • Slow Burn • Turbo Rock.
00001076 Book/CD Pack.................................$9.95

BLUES CRUISE

Mid-Intermediate Level
by Dave Rubin

Blues Cruise features 10 original songs with bluesy chords, rhythms, and riffs. Includes: Delta Catfish • Detroit Boogie • Hill Country Stomp • Houston Shuffle • Kansas City Swing • Louisiana Gumbo • Memphis Soul • Southside Man • West Coast Strut • Westside Minor Groove.
00000470 Book/CD Pack.................................$9.95

MYSTERIOSO

Mid-Intermediate Level
by Allan Jaffe

Mysterioso features 10 original songs with spooky melodies and riffs. Includes: The Chase • A Daunting Haunting • The Disappearing Guests • The Galloping Nightmare • Guitar Noir • The Gumshoe's Smooth Move • Mysterioso • The Plot Thickens • The Secret Panel • Skeleton Dance.
00000471 Book/CD Pack.................................$9.95

Essential Elements Guitar Songs

The books in the Essential Elements Guitar Songs series feature popular songs arranged for a specific approach to playing the guitar. Each book/CD pack includes eight great songs.

POWER CHORD ROCK

Mid-Beginner Level

Songs include: All the Small Things • I Love Rock 'N Roll • I Won't Back Down • Mony, Mony • Self Esteem • Smells like Teen Spirit • Talk Dirty to Me • You Really Got Me.
00001139 Book/CD Pack.................................$12.95

OPEN CHORD ROCK

Mid-Beginner Level

Songs include: Brown Eyed Girl • Bye Bye Love • Don't Be Cruel (To a Heart That's True) • Have You Ever Seen the Rain? • Learning to Fly • Love Me Do • Should I Stay or Should I Go • Willie and the Hand Jive.
00001138 Book/CD Pack.................................$12.95

BARRE CHORD ROCK

Late Beginner Level

Songs include: All Along the Watchtower • I Can't Explain • Nowhere Man • (Sittin' On) The Dock of the Bay • Stray Cat Strut • Summer of '69 • Surrender • Wild Thing.
00001137 Book/CD Pack.................................$12.95

FOR MORE INFORMATION,
SEE YOUR LOCAL MUSIC DEALER,
OR WRITE TO:

HAL•LEONARD®
CORPORATION
7777 W. BLUEMOUND RD. P.O. BOX 13819
MILWAUKEE, WISCONSIN 53213

Prices, contents, and availability subject to change without notice.